YOUNG DISCOVERERS

For Liberty, with love - S.D.

To Matilda, my courageous and wonderful adventurer - V. L.

———————

Young Discoverers © 2026 Quarto Publishing plc.
Text © 2026 Stephen Davies. Illustrations © 2026 Violaine Leroy

First published in 2026 by Wide Eyed Editions, an imprint of The Quarto Group.
100 Cummings Center, Suite 265D, Beverly, MA 01915, USA.
T (978) 282-9590 F (978) 283-2742 www.Quarto.com
EEA Representation, WTS Tax d.o.o., Žanova ulica 3, 4000 Kranj, Slovenia.

A catalog record for this book is available from the British Library.

ISBN 978-0-7112-9830-9

The illustrations were created digitally.
Set in Cormorant, Fabiola Capitals and Neutraface 2 Text.

Designers: Sasha Moxon and Melissa Gandhi
Editors: Hannah Dove, Katie Taylor and Leah Baxter
Production Manager: Robin Boothroyd
Aquisitions Editor: Hannah Dove
Art Director: Karissa Santos
Publisher: Debbie Foy

Manufactured in Guangdong, China TT102025

9 8 7 6 5 4 3 2 1

YOUNG DISCOVERERS

WRITTEN BY
STEPHEN DAVIES

ILLUSTRATED BY
VIOLAINE LEROY

WIDE EYED EDITIONS

CONTENTS

WELCOME, FUTURE DISCOVERERS!

Golden statues, mysterious scrolls, fossilized bones of fantastical creatures . . . Have you ever dreamed of discovering something extraordinary? The children and teenagers in this book did exactly that.

Some made their discoveries in secret tunnels or on jagged cliff faces. Others were simply going about their everyday lives when they noticed something unusual, something that led them to take a closer look.

Many followed their senses to their big discovery—whether it was seeing something that looked out of place, feeling something strange against their fingers, or hearing an unexpected sound. One even followed his nose to an incredible find.

Within these pages you will meet young discoverers between the ages of four and eighteen. Different people, different places, different times in history, but they all had one thing in common: they were curious about the world around them.

If the stories in this book seem like adventure fiction, keep reminding yourself that they really are true. We researched these stories using newspaper articles and, wherever possible, eyewitness reports. People's accounts of the same events do sometimes vary, but we have pieced our versions together as best we can, for you to enjoy.

Prepare to be inspired by these amazing true tales, and remember to keep your eyes, ears, and nostrils wide open. Every time you wake up in the morning, a groundbreaking discovery could be waiting for you.

Who knows what treasures are still waiting to be unearthed? Or better still, waiting for you to unearth them . . .

CONRAD REED

STRIKES GOLD

LITTLE MEADOW CREEK IN
NORTH CAROLINA, UNITED
STATES OF AMERICA, 1799

One warm Sunday morning in spring, a twelve-year-old boy named Conrad was running along the bank of a stream, clutching a homemade bow and arrow. His older sister Frances jogged behind, hand in hand with their little brother George.

"Slow down, Conrad!" Frances yelled.

"Shhh!" Conrad scowled at his sister. "You'll scare the fish away!"

Conrad had woken up extra early that morning. He had milked the cows, collected the eggs, fetched three pails of water, and brushed Adalard, the family horse, from mane to hoof. As a reward, he was now allowed some time away from his endless list of chores—two blissful hours fishing in the stream that ran through the family farm.

While he waited for Frances and George to catch up, Conrad nocked an arrow and peered down at the babbling water in the creek. A dozen minnows sped by, but Conrad was not interested in minnows. This morning, only a plump perch would do.

There! A flash of yellow! Quick!

Conrad's arrow flew fast and true. He splashed down into the creek and reached for his prize.

But what he drew out of the water was not a shiny yellow perch.

It was a shiny yellow rock.

The rock was wedge-shaped and extremely heavy. No good for dinner, of course, but not a bad find for first thing in the morning.

John and Sarah Reed returned home from church to find Conrad, Frances, and George waiting for them. Conrad thrust the yellow rock into his father's hand. "I found this down at the creek," he said.

"Wow!" his dad exclaimed. "Look how sparkly it is. And heavy, too. What on earth could it be?"

John Reed had a feeling that Conrad's rock might be special in some way. He wrapped it in a piece of burlap and tucked it into a gap in the wall of their cabin to keep it safe. There it stayed for three whole years, almost forgotten about as life on the farm carried on. Almost forgotten, but not entirely.

Early one morning, John Reed was saddling Adalard to go to a faraway town on business, when his wife called out to him, "Why don't you take that lump of shining stuff with you, and see if anyone knows what it is?"

All day long, Conrad waited impatiently for his father to return. As soon as he heard the faint clip-clop of hooves, he rushed outside.

"Gold!" his father yelled. "The first gold ever found in America, the jeweler said! He turned your lump of rock into a solid gold bar seven inches long, and told me to name my price!"

Conrad's mouth dropped open. "And?"

"Three dollars and fifty cents!" His father punched the air.

"I spent it on a dress for your mother, a shoulder of beef, and a bag of strange-looking beans from the Caribbean. Coffee, it's called. I've heard it's delicious."

As it turned out, the coffee beans were a disappointment. Conrad's mom cooked them with the beef, and the resulting stew was so disgusting that no one ate more than a spoonful.

An even bigger disappointment came a few days later, when Conrad heard his father talking with a local preacher named James Love. "I hate to tell you this," said Mr. Love, "but that gold you sold was actually worth a thousand times that price."

Conrad's father hardly ever got angry, but this news made him slam his fist on the table so hard that little George burst into tears.

John Reed realized that there was probably more gold on his land, but his experience with the jeweler had taught him not to go it alone. He invited three friends to join him as business partners: his brother-in-law Frederick Kiser, the preacher Mr. Love, and a wealthy landowner named Martin Kiser. They would search for gold on John's land and would split any profits equally between them.

This was 1803, long before slavery was abolished in America. People from West Africa and the Caribbean were kidnapped from their home countries, then bought and sold as if they were possessions. Mr. Love, Mr. Phifer and Mr. Kiser sent enslaved people to work in Little Meadow Creek, swirling water and gravel from the creek bed one pan at a time. It was slow, backbreaking work.

In late summer, an enslaved man named Peter spotted a nugget of gold weighing twenty-eight pounds, a full eleven pounds heavier than the nugget young Conrad had found in 1799.

Peter's nugget sold for $6,600. John Reed and his overjoyed business partners each received $1,650. Peter himself received nothing.

News of gold spreads fast. Conrad and Peter's discoveries
sparked a gold rush in North Carolina, with businesspeople,
miners, and merchants from all over the world flocking to the
area to seek their fortune. Over the fifty years that followed,
millions of dollars' worth of gold would be unearthed.

The gold rush was bad news for the American Indians in the area,
many of whom were forced to leave their lands. The miners also damaged
the environment, blocking streams, cutting down trees, and ruining
farmland.

As a teenager growing up during a gold rush and witnessing
its consequences, how did Conrad feel about his discovery
in the creek? Did he ever wish he had found a fish instead?

We can only imagine.

MARY ANNING

UNEARTHS A SEA MONSTER

LYME REGIS, ENGLAND, 1811

Waves crashed and the wind blew hard as seagulls swooped overhead. A twelve-year-old girl named Mary clambered over a mass of limestone boulders on Charmouth Beach, her treasure-hunting gaze flickering across the surface of each rock.

The treasure Mary sought was not gold or silver but "thunderbolts," "verteberries," and "snake stones": secret curiosities from a lost world hiding inside the rocks right there on the beach. Tourists would buy them for a penny each at the little stall outside her house. Since Father died, Mother needed those pennies more than ever.

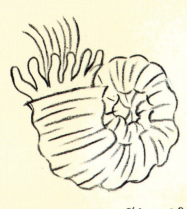

Snake Stones

Mary's superstitious neighbors wore these tightly coiled fossils as protection against snake bites. We now know them as ammonites, the remains of mollusks which lived in the ocean at the time of the dinosaurs.

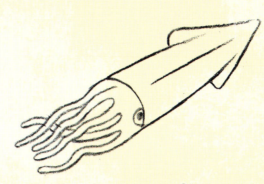

Thunderbolts

These pointy stones are now called "belemnites." Each one was once the beak of a prehistoric squid.

Verteberries

Mary's neighbors knew that these chunky discs came from giants' backbones, but they never suspected that those giants were reptiles or that they swam through our oceans millions of years ago.

Mary's older brother Joseph was further up the beach. "Hey, Mary!" he shouted suddenly. "What do you think of this?"

When Mary saw what her brother had found, she gasped out loud. It looked for all the world like a giant, stony eye, staring out at them from inside a rock.

The children carted the rock back home and chiseled away at it with their father's tools. As the hours passed, a pile of gravel rose around their feet. When they finally finished, they stepped back, staring in awe at an enormous, grinning skull.

"It's a crocodile," Joseph said.

"Nonsense." Mary's brow furrowed. "No crocodile has eyes that big."

Mary was determined to find the rest of the monster. For eleven long months she scoured the beach, trudging through wind and rain, digging through shale and small stones, probing and prodding until her eyes ached and her fingers bled.

Her perseverance paid off. Deep in the sand at the foot of the cliff, Mary finally found a tangle of curved ribs, knobby vertebrae, and smooth flipper bones. This had to be the missing body, and it was so enormous, she felt dizzy just looking at it!

The skeleton was like nothing anyone had ever seen. Mary's mother sold it to a local landowner, who donated it to a London museum. The huge, empty eye gazed out from its glass case and crowds of visitors goggled back at it.

Many Christian people at the time took the Bible very literally, and believed that Earth was only 6,000 years old. If this was the case, then how had Mary's monster ended up buried beneath so many layers of solid rock?

Famous scientists were just as puzzled. What was this thing? A fish? A lizard? Some kind of dragon from old folktales?

Mary's discovery was given the name ichthyosaur, which means "fish-lizard." We now know that it swam in the ocean 200 million years ago, when dinosaurs roamed the land.

Mary's discovery spurred her on to even greater efforts. By day she searched the cliffs and beaches near her home, and by night she pored over complicated books, learning everything she could about animals and rocks. This young girl, whose family had no money to send her to school, was becoming a world expert in the brand-new science of paleontology (the study of fossils).

By the age of twenty-seven, Mary had saved up enough money to open her very own fossil shop, which was visited by tourists, scientists, and even royalty. She continued discovering fossils too, including another marine reptile from 200 million years ago. It was given the name plesiosaur, meaning "almost-lizard," and it was even bigger and stranger looking than the ichthyosaur!

Two hundred years ago, science was thought to be a subject for men, not women, so Mary was never properly rewarded for her work. However, her discoveries of long-extinct creatures did change the way people thought, helping them realize that Earth was not thousands of years old, but hundreds of millions of years old.

Children and adults all over the world have been inspired by Mary Anning's story, her discoveries, and her relentless passion for learning.

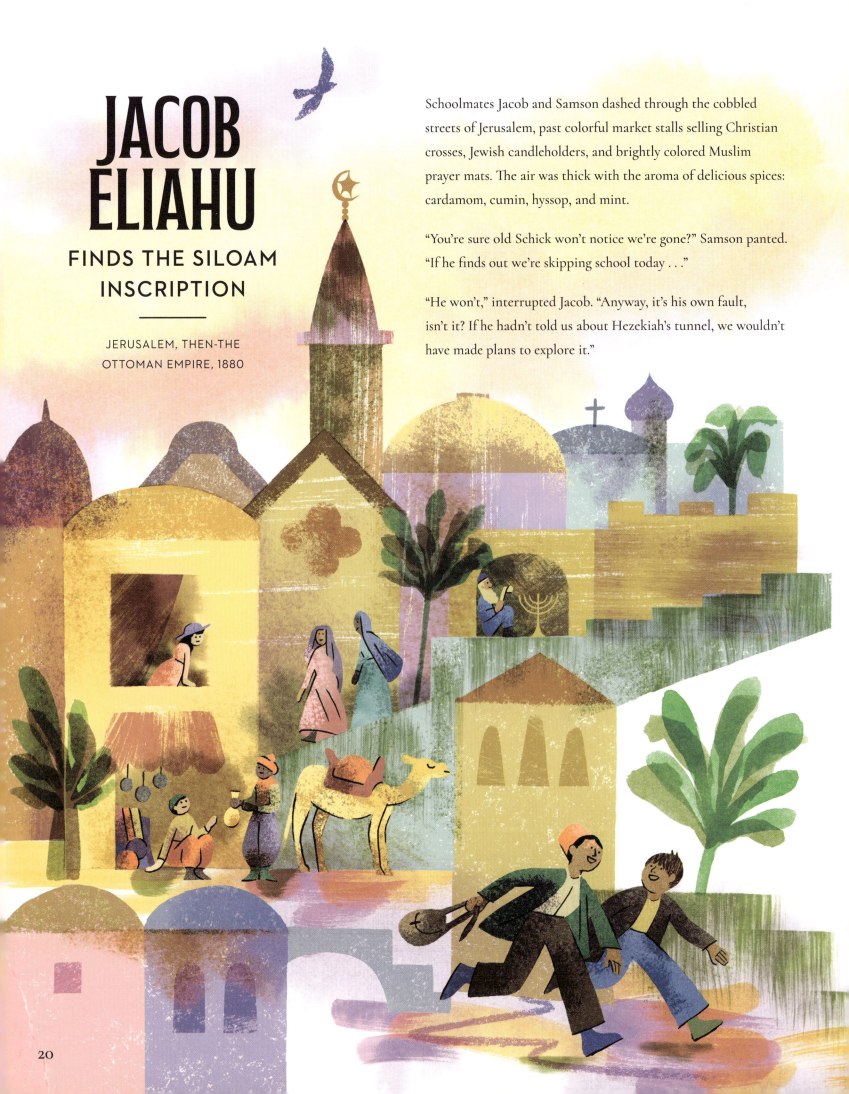

JACOB ELIAHU

FINDS THE SILOAM INSCRIPTION

JERUSALEM, THEN-THE
OTTOMAN EMPIRE, 1880

Schoolmates Jacob and Samson dashed through the cobbled streets of Jerusalem, past colorful market stalls selling Christian crosses, Jewish candleholders, and brightly colored Muslim prayer mats. The air was thick with the aroma of delicious spices: cardamom, cumin, hyssop, and mint.

"You're sure old Schick won't notice we're gone?" Samson panted. "If he finds out we're skipping school today . . ."

"He won't," interrupted Jacob. "Anyway, it's his own fault, isn't it? If he hadn't told us about Hezekiah's tunnel, we wouldn't have made plans to explore it."

Conrad Schick was the headmaster of Jacob and Samson's school, and he had told them an incredible tale in history class last week. The story went like this:

In the year 701 BCE, King Hezekiah of Jerusalem received news that a terrifying army from Assyria was planning to attack his city. Hezekiah knew he had no chance of beating them in battle, so he decided to use cunning instead.

He ordered his workers to dig a tunnel under Jerusalem, causing the nearby spring of Gihon to flow into the city rather than out of it.

When the Assyrian soldiers and horses arrived, there was nothing for them to drink outside the city walls. Not a drop! After a miserable two-month standoff, the thirsty Assyrians agreed to go away, in return for a gift of gold and silver.

Schick had shown them the story in the Bible, and had described the route of the tunnel from the spring of Gihon to the Pool of Siloam almost half a mile away. Jacob couldn't believe that the very tunnel from the story was right beneath his feet, just waiting to be explored!

Leaving the marketplace far behind them, Jacob and Samson scrambled down a grassy bank, which in Hezekiah's day marked the southern edge of Jerusalem.

"We'll split up," Jacob said. "You enter the tunnel at the Gihon end, I'll enter at Siloam and we'll meet in the middle."

"Will we?" Samson muttered darkly. "My mom says the tunnel is guarded by a powerful demon!"

Arriving at the pool of Siloam, Jacob took from his bag a cork float, four candles, some matches, and a strip of sandpaper.

"There is no tunnel demon," he said out loud, eyeing the pitch-black opening ahead of him. "There is no tunnel demon."

Jacob took a deep breath and lowered himself into the muddy water, gasping at the sudden cold. He steadied his trembling fingers, lit the candles, and melted the ends to attach them to the corners of his float.

As the schoolboy crept cautiously into the tunnel, the water began to rise around him. First up to his waist . . .

then to his chest . . .

and then right up to his neck . . .

"There is no tunnel demon," he stammered, forcing himself to keep moving forward. "There is no tunnel demon . . . there is no—"

Jacob stumbled and lurched forward into the water. The float flipped over and the candles went out, plunging him into total darkness . . .

SPLASH!

At the other end of the tunnel, at the spring of Gihon, a small boy was filling a clay jar. Suddenly a wild-eyed, mud-caked figure burst up out of the water at his feet and seized him by the shoulders.

The boy shrieked with terror, convinced that the tunnel demon from the stories had finally come to capture him. The boy's mother dashed forward and swiped him up on to the bank. As the muddy water settled, it was not a demon they saw in front of them, but Jacob, dripping from head to toe.

"Forgive me," Jacob said, his eyes sparkling with excitement. "I thought your son was my friend Samson. I've found something amazing in the tunnel. I need to go and tell old Schick!"

Back at the school, Jacob found Samson, who had chickened out of entering the tunnel at the last minute. He also found his headmaster.

"Sir, sir!" Jacob gasped. "I was in Hezekiah's tunnel, feeling my way along the wall in the darkness, when I felt some sort of writing. I think it might be Hebrew."

Jacob's guess was correct. When Conrad Schick investigated, he found an astonishing inscription on the wall of the tunnel, dating from the time of Hezekiah himself. It told the story of how the king's workers had dug the tunnel in two teams, starting from both ends and meeting in the middle.

As the oldest example of Biblical Hebrew ever discovered, the inscription caused much excitement in Jerusalem. In 1890, a thief entered the tunnel and hacked the priceless inscription off the wall, breaking it in the process. Thankfully, it was recovered a year later. It was taken to Istanbul in Turkey, where it remains to this day.

As for Jacob, he went on to become an expert in archaeology, leading guided tours around all sorts of sites mentioned in the Bible. On his tours, he would often tell the story of how the Siloam inscription was discovered by a schoolboy, but he'd leave out the most important detail of all: that the schoolboy was him!

HUSSEIN ABDEL-RASSOUL

UNCOVERS A PHARAOH'S TOMB

QURNA, EGYPT, 1922

A donkey plodded through the Valley of the Kings, past the tombs of long-lost pharaohs and the shrine of a local holy man, Abd el-Qurna. On the donkey's back, a young boy swayed from side to side, his tongue clicking to urge the animal forward.

The sun had barely risen above the eastern horizon, but work in the valley was already underway. Hussein heard the chatter of Qurnawi basket boys, the barked commands of the boss, Ahmed Gerigar, and the clang of pickax heads on ancient limestone. This was the site of an archaeological dig, and the workers were looking for something very special.

As soon as Hussein reached the workers, he hopped down, loosened the slip-knot on his donkey's saddle, and took the weight of the water jar in his arms.

"Found a tomb yet?" he called to his friend Mamoud, who was grunting as he piled rubble into his basket.

"Give us a chance," Mamoud laughed. "This is only our third day of digging."

"Third day of digging this year, you mean." Hussein scuffed his bare heel into the sand to make a hole for the water jar. "There was also last year, and the year before that, and the year before that, and the—"

He broke off suddenly, staring at the ground.

"Hussein, your water!" Mamoud yelled as the clay jar leaned over, almost in slow motion, then toppled and cracked.

Hussein ignored his friend and the broken jar. He was down on his knees, combing frantically through the sand to uncover something smooth and white.

A stone.

No, a slab.

No, a step!

If there was one step, might there be more hiding in the earth?
And where could they possibly lead? Hussein's heart skipped a beat and his imagination filled with pictures of tunnels, tombs, and priceless treasures.

When Hussein returned home that night, he found his mother making flatbread.

"I found it, Mom!" the young boy yelled. "I found it!"

"I didn't know it was missing," his mother murmured. "Tie it up, quick, before you lose it again."

"Not the donkey, Mom, a tomb!"

"What?" His mother stopped rolling the dough and looked sternly up at him.

"I found the first step of a tomb, as smooth and white as goat's milk. I showed Mamoud, and Mamoud showed Gerigar, and Gerigar said to wait for Carter, so we all sat down and waited for an hour—"

"'Hussein, slow down!"

"—and when Carter finally arrived and saw the step, his eyes went all wide and his mustache started to quiver. He told the axe men to dig-dig-dig! They uncovered another step, and another, and another, until there were twelve steps leading down into the ground. Twelve steps, Mom, and a sealed door with hieroglyphs and everything!"

"Whose tomb is it, Hussein? Was there a name on the door?"

"I don't know. They filled it all in again with earth. For protection, Gerigar said."

"What are they waiting for?"

"For a rich man to arrive from England. They said he has to be here when the workers open the tomb."

"Why?"

"I don't know. Gerigar didn't say."

The waiting was almost unbearable. It took three whole weeks for the man to arrive, and another two days before he and Carter were ready to open the tomb.

"Patience is the head of wisdom," Hussein's mother kept saying, but the old proverb did nothing to calm Hussein's excitement and anxiety. Would they find treasure in the tomb, or had it already been looted by ancient tomb robbers?

After what felt like forever, the day finally came. On November 26, 1922, Hussein watched with bated breath as the two Englishmen disappeared into the mysterious tomb with Gerigar. It took a long time for them to emerge, but when they did, Carter's face was shining like the saintly Abd el-Qurna himself.

The wondrous news spread fast among the workers. "It's the tomb of the boy-king Tutankhamun!" they called to each other, "and it's full to bursting with gold!"

"And much, much more!" Gerigar beamed. "Chariots, weapons, jewelry, clothes—it's all there! It's like a messenger from the past has come and told us everything we ever wanted to know about the life of an Egyptian pharaoh."

Years of hard work followed. Five thousand pieces of treasure were brought out of the tomb, photographed, cataloged, and transported to the Egyptian Museum in Cairo. Hussein and his donkey played their part, of course, supplying water to thirsty workers every day.

In November 1926, the official tomb photographer Harry Burton called Hussein to pose for a photo wearing one of Tutankhamun's own necklaces. Hussein marveled at the weight of the gold across his shoulders and the brightness of the precious stones that flashed and sparkled in the sun. A sudden thought made his head swim. *"When Tutankhamun was my age, he was the ruler of all of Egypt!"*

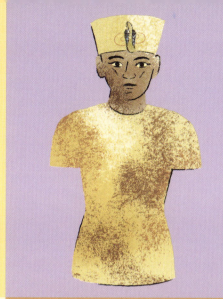

The necklace ended up in the Egyptian Museum with the rest of the treasure, but Hussein received a copy of the photograph as a thank you for his contribution to one of the most incredible discoveries ever known. He kept that photograph all his life.

ROY SPENCER

DISCOVERS THE WORLD'S BIGGEST STAR SAPPHIRE

QUEENSLAND,
AUSTRALIA, 1937

On a scorching summer day in Queensland, Australia, an eleven-year-old boy was digging in a dry, rocky riverbed. All of a sudden, he leapt up and ran to the desert oak tree where his family was having a picnic. "Look, Dad, I found something!"

Harry Spencer glanced at the rock in his son's hand. "It's worthless, Roy. Just black crystal."

"I thought it might be a sapphire," said Roy, disappointed.

Roy's older brother Lance could never pass up an opportunity to tease the baby of the family. "Black sapphires don't exist, you fool. Sapphires are blue, green, or yellow, everyone knows that."

"Do you think this might be a sapphire?" cackled another brother, waving a gnawed chicken bone above his head.

Harry Spencer caught his wife's eye and resisted the urge to laugh. He remembered all too well how tough it could feel, being an eleven year old surrounded by all-knowing adults. Eleven was the exact age at which he had lost his mother and taken over her sapphire business.

Harry put down his sandwich and took the crystal in both hands. "You know what, son?" he said, more gently this time. "It'll make a doozy of a doorstop."

Life carried on for the Spencers. Ten years passed and no one gave a second thought to the lump of black rock lying near the door.

That was until an eagle-eyed gemstone buyer visited. "Is that what I think it is?" he asked, staring at the doorstop.

"It's just crystal," Harry replied.

Harry sounded confident, but in truth the buyer's question had unsettled him. At closing time, he took a piece of quartz and scraped it hard against the doorstop. If the doorstop was worthless crystal, the quartz would leave a deep scratch on it.

To Harry's amazement, the exact opposite happened. The doorstop scratched the quartz!

"Roy, you have to look at this!" he shouted. "It turns out that black sapphires do exist! And you found an absolutely humungous one!"

Harry Spencer sold the doorstop for $18,000, enough money to build a new house. And while the family was moving into their beautiful new home, the black sapphire was also on the move.

The sapphire's next owner, gem cutter Harry Kazanjian, took it halfway across the world to a fifth-floor workshop in downtown New York. Once there, he studied it for weeks, trying to imagine the jewel inside the rough.

Finally, he was ready to grind.

Harry's nephew Michael was visiting him that summer. Michael was eleven years old, exactly the same age Roy had been when he made his amazing discovery. He stood and watched open-mouthed as his uncle hunched over the grinding wheel.

"I'm going to make a smooth, curved jewel called a cabochon," Uncle Harry explained. "Wish me luck, Michael."

The grinding wheel was made of copper and plated with diamond dust. Diamond is even harder than sapphire, and as soon as the sapphire touched the wheel, pieces of black grit began to fly.

"Are you nervous, Uncle?" Michael whispered.

"A little," Harry admitted. "This beauty cost me a lot of money, and one mistake now could completely ruin it."

The grinding and polishing took months of careful work, but the end result was even more beautiful than Michael could have imagined. The sapphire was jet black and glossy, with a six-pointed star shining out from the middle.

When his uncle passed it to him, Michael couldn't believe how heavy it felt and how bright the inner star was. "It's like holding the whole universe between your finger and thumb," he gasped.

Daily News

October 6th, 1938

Gem Owner Stops Using Sapphires as Doorstops

At 733 carats, it was the biggest star sapphire the world had ever seen. Photos appeared in newspapers all over the world, including Australia.

"Look Dad, we're famous!" said Roy Spencer, showing his father the headline in the *Brisbane Telegraph*. "They've named it 'the Black Star of Queensland'!"

The Black Star of Queensland had formed deep underground over billions of years, completely hidden from view. Thanks to Roy Spencer and Harry Kazanjian, it was now in the public eye. Film stars and fashion models were photographed holding the stone and it even appeared on TV, hanging around the neck of one of the world's best-selling singers, Cher.

Two Stars

SAPPHIRE A GOOD LUCK CHARM

★ THE NEW YOR

Romance and the Stone

By 1950, the sapphire was thought to be worth a whopping $300,000. Michael felt a strong connection to the sapphire. He used to visit it in the high security vault where it was kept, and talk to it about his hopes and dreams for the future. "It has a lovely personality," he used to tell people. "Very dramatic. Very powerful."

Michael Kazanjian and Roy Spencer both ended up becoming gem cutters themselves. They were devoted to their craft, cutting and polishing some of the finest jewels in the world.

And nowadays, even fools know that not all sapphires are blue, yellow, or green—they can also be a stunning, cosmic black.

MARCEL RAVIDAT

FINDS PREHISTORIC CAVE PAINTINGS

—

MONTIGNAC, FRANCE, 1940

Marcel was eighteen and he worked as a mechanic's apprentice in a French village called Montignac. When he wasn't busy repairing cars, Marcel would walk in the nearby forests with his dog, Robot.

One Tuesday morning, Robot was even more excited than usual—chasing his tail, doing somersaults in the air, and shooting off to investigate even the faintest of rustles in the undergrowth.

"Come back, you big goofball!" cried Marcel as Robot bounded into the bushes for the hundredth time.

As Marcel hurried after his little terrier, he stumbled on a loose stone, knocking it into a hole beside an uprooted pine tree. But to his surprise, the stone didn't stop there. It kept falling and falling, its echoes calling back to Marcel from deeper and deeper underground. Until finally, it landed with a . . . CLACK!

Marcel could not stop thinking about the sound the stone had made, and two days later he returned to investigate. On his way, he met three younger boys: sixteen-year-old Georges, fifteen-year-old Jacques, and fourteen-year-old Simon.

"Hey Marcel," said Jacques. "Where are you off to?"

"Underground!" Marcel grinned. "I found a deep hole and I want to see where it leads."

The younger boys looked at the lamps and shovel in Marcel's hands. They sensed straight away that adventure was in store. "Can we come?" they pleaded.

"Sure! You can help me widen the entrance."

Marcel led the way to the hole, and they began to clear out rocks, shrubs, old animal bones, and shards of broken glass.

"Local legend says there's a tunnel under the forest," Jacques said. "It connects Lascaux Manor with Montignac Castle."

"I've heard that too!" Georges cried. "My nana says it's full of TREASURE CHESTS!"

After an hour of hard work, the hole was just wide enough for Marcel's shoulders. He took a deep breath, knelt down, and wriggled headfirst into the gap.

"It's a tight squeeze!" he called back to the others. "Pitch-black, too."

Marcel edged forward a little farther. Forward . . . forward . . . forward . . . until . . .

"Aargh, someone grab my feet, quick! I'm going to fall!"

Marcel landed on a pile of rocks in the darkness.

He sat up, lit his kerosene lamp, and looked around. Wherever he was, it was actually quite spacious, more like a cave than a tunnel. He ignored the scrapes from his fall and began to edge farther away from the entrance, his heart pounding in his chest.

Oof! Eesh! Bof! The younger lads clattered down into the cave behind Marcel.

"Wait for us, Marcel!" called Georges.

"I hope there aren't bats in here," Simon stammered.

As the younger boys crawled toward him, Marcel stood up, lit a second lamp, and raised it high above his head.

The sight that met his eyes was so stunning and unexpected that he staggered backward, unable to take it in.

Red and ochre, black and white, the boys were surrounded by painted animals so lifelike that they seemed to buck and stampede across the walls and ceilings.

"DEER!"

"HORSES! BULLS!"

"WOAH!!!"

"What is this place? It's incredible!"

At first, the boys swore to keep their find a secret. They explored a little farther every day, whooping and cheering at each new incredible discovery. There were seven interconnected chambers and hundreds of paintings of wild animals.

In the end, the secret was simply too big to keep. The first adult they invited into the cave was their old schoolteacher, Leon Laval. "Boys, this is magnificent!" he cried, gaping at the bisons, stags, and charging rhinos. "These are from the Stone Age!"

Next came Henri Breuil, a true expert in prehistory. It was Henri who revealed to the boys just how significant their discovery really was.

"Do you realize how ancient this artwork is? The Pyramids of Giza are 5,000 years old, but this stag is 17,000 years old!"

"See how the back legs of these bison are crossing each other! What a skillful artist!"

"They used charcoal for black, berries for red, and wet clay for brown and ochre. Such vivid colors, even now! The best-preserved cave paintings in the world!"

"Aurochs! It's an extinct species of cow. We only knew about them from fossils . . . until today!"

"I've studied prehistory all my life, but I have NO IDEA what I'm looking at here!"

Marcel and Jacques pitched a tent outside the cave and remained there throughout the winter to welcome visitors. Hundreds of tourists and journalists lined up to witness the finest examples of prehistoric art ever discovered.

World War II soon halted the adventure, but Marcel, Georges, Jacques, and Simon all survived the war and lived long and interesting lives. On the forty-sixth anniversary of their discovery—and every year after that—they reunited at the Lascaux caves to whoop and cheer once again.

MUHAMMAD AHMED AL-HAMED

DISCOVERS HIDDEN MANUSCRIPTS FROM ANCIENT TIMES

QUMRAN, JORDAN, 1947

A young Bedouin shepherd named Muhammad trudged downhill toward the shore of the Dead Sea. His feet ached, his sandals were coming apart at the seams, and his throat was as dry as dust. He longed for a drink of water, and to see Juma again.

"Well?" Cousin Juma greeted him with a smile and a water pouch. "Did you find your goat?"

"No." Muhammad drank deeply and passed the skin back. "Fifty-five goats have become fifty-four goats. My father will be furious when we get home next week." Muhammad sat down on a rock to rest. "I did find something else, though," he said at last. "The opening of a cave, almost ten feet above the ground. I threw a stone in, hoping to hear the goat bleat or move . . . but instead I heard a quiet crash, like a clay pot was breaking down there."

"Wow." Juma's eyes widened. "I'll bet you ran away, like you'd seen a ghost!"

"Of course not," Muhammad lied.

That night, the young shepherd could not sleep. He kept thinking about the sound he had heard. What kind of person leaves clay pots in a cave? And then it came to him. Someone hiding gold, that's who.

When morning finally came, Muhammad returned to the cave, this time with Juma.

"Higher," Muhammad croaked, balancing precariously on his cousin's hands. "Higher. Higher. There!"

He hooked his fingertips over the edge of the entrance and pulled himself up, biceps burning with the strain. He slithered through the gap and down into the cave beyond.

As his eyes adjusted to the gloom, he noticed ten clay jars standing in a line.

Could they be filled with treasure?

Muhammad leapt forward to find out.

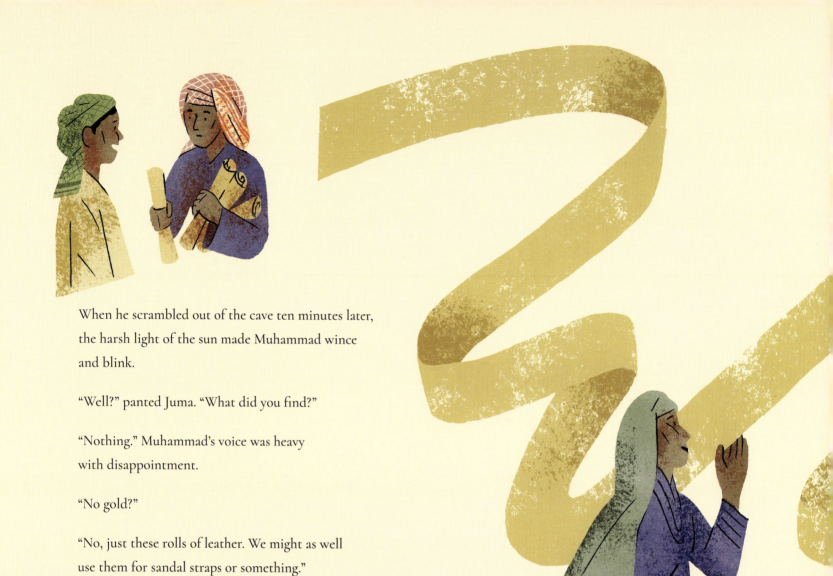

When he scrambled out of the cave ten minutes later, the harsh light of the sun made Muhammad wince and blink.

"Well?" panted Juma. "What did you find?"

"Nothing." Muhammad's voice was heavy with disappointment.

"No gold?"

"No, just these rolls of leather. We might as well use them for sandal straps or something."

A few days later, the boys and their flocks arrived back at their family's tent. Muhammad's father was mad about the lost goat, but he forgot his anger when he saw the leather scrolls. They were covered in writing that the family didn't recognize, and the biggest one stretched all the way from one end of the tent to the other.

Uncle Khalil was even more intrigued. "The leather is far too brittle for sandal repairs," he said, "but the writing may be of interest to someone."

For several weeks, the bundle of leather hung from the pole in the middle of the family tent. Smaller children in the family played with one of the scrolls, tearing it clean in two.

A couple of months later, the shepherds showed the scrolls to an antiques dealer in the city of Bethlehem, who suggested they take them to the Syrian monastery in Jerusalem.

The monk at the monastery gate was not expecting a visit from a group of Bedouin shepherds brandishing rolls of old leather. He shook his fist at them and chased them away. Thankfully, the shepherds returned two weeks later and saw a different monk, who paid them sixteen Palestinian pounds for their scrolls. The shepherds went home happy, knowing that those green and yellow banknotes would buy at least twenty-five goats at the market in Bethlehem.

Monks and scholars assembled at a local university, and huddled around a kerosene lamp to unroll the biggest scroll. They gasped out loud when they realized that it contained the words of the Hebrew prophet Isaiah. With trembling fingers, they compared the ancient scroll with the book of Isaiah in their own Hebrew Bible. The two versions were exactly the same, word for word!

Over the months and years that followed, hundreds
more "Dead Sea Scrolls" were discovered in the region.
They included almost all of the books in the Hebrew Bible,
including the famous stories of Adam and Eve, Moses and
Pharaoh, David and Goliath, and Noah's Ark. Scholars were in
disbelief when they dated the scrolls and found that they were a
thousand years older than any other Bible in existence. For Jews
and Christians all over the world, those scruffy pieces of leather
proved more precious than any amount of gold or silver.

As for the young discoverer, he became known among the
Bedouin people as Muhammed edh-Dhib—Muhammed the
Wolf—on account of the courage he had shown in wriggling
head first into a pitch-black cave!

MATTHEW BERGER

STUMBLES UPON A NOT-QUITE-HUMAN SKELETON

MALAPA, SOUTH AFRICA, 2008

Lee Berger was a paleontologist, a type of scientist who studies fossils. One morning, he parked his car on a sun-baked hill and grinned at his colleague, Job Kibii.

"I'm hoping for some good finds today," he said.

Lee's nine-year-old son Matt had come along for the adventure, and so had Tau, their energetic Rhodesian Ridgeback. As soon as Matt's dad opened the trunk, Tau leapt down and scampered off, with Matt following him.

To the east, a curly-horned antelope was grazing. The dog paused to watch it for a few seconds but didn't give chase.

"Good boy, Tau!" Matt called. "You wouldn't hurt a fly, would you?"

Tau bounded off down a narrow track, away from the antelope.

"Wait for me!" Matt yelled.

The boy broke into a run, speeding after Tau. He didn't see the tree root in front of him until it was too late.

"Yeow!" Matt staggered a few paces, then landed headfirst in the long grass.

As Matt brushed the dirt off his jeans, he spotted something nearby—a large lump of clay with a pale ridge sticking out.

"Dad!" he called. "I've found a fossilized bone!"

The adults came running over. "Already?" Matt's dad chuckled. "We've only been here ninety seconds!" As soon as his dad caught sight of the bone, the chuckling stopped and the shouting started.

"Hominid!" he kept yelling. "Hominid! Hominid!"

The word hominid means any kind of ape or human, but Matt didn't know that at the time. Baffled by the shouting, he thought his dad was angry about something.

But Lee Berger was not angry, not in the slightest; he was thrilled and flabbergasted. "Congratulations, Matty!" he cried. "You just found the collarbone of a prehistoric human ancestor!"

51

In the car on the way home, Lee, Job, and Matt talked about evolution. Millions of years ago, some apes started to develop bigger brains and shorter tails, and began to walk upright. By 300,000 years ago, these super-sophisticated apes looked very much like us. Fossils of these extinct hominids are fascinating because they prove the existence of weird and wonderful "in between" species that were ape-like in some ways and human-like in others.

The rest of Matt's hominid was eventually unearthed. The scientists who examined the fossilized skeleton concluded that it belonged to a nine-to-thirteen-year-old boy who lived two million years ago! This boy walked on two feet but was also an amazing climber, using his super-strong fingers to swing effortlessly up and down trees.

A competition was held to find a nickname for the prehistoric boy Matt had discovered. The winner was seventeen-year-old Omphemetse Keepile, who suggested her own sister's name, Karabo, meaning "solution" in the Tswana language of South Africa. "This fossil represents a solution toward understanding the origins of humankind," she explained.

Omphemetse and Matt became almost as famous as Karabo himself.

FIVE YEARS LATER . . .

One fall evening, Matt (who was now fourteen years old) was relaxing at home, reading a thrilling story about ancient Greek monsters. Suddenly, two visitors knocked on the door. They were cavers, wanting to see his dad.

"We found a narrow crack at the back of the Rising Star cave system," said one. "It leads down to a chamber full of bones."

"We think the bones might be prehistoric," said the other.

Matt's dad needed detailed scientific photos of the bones, but he knew there was no way he could fit down the crack. "Hey, Matt." He winked at his son. "Want to go caving?"

The teenager grinned. "Always."

The shaft was only seven inches wide at its narrowest point, but Matt was slim and skillful enough to squirm down.

The chamber below was littered with hominid bones! Matt trembled with excitement. It was a while before his hands were still enough to take the photos they needed.

Matt's dad sent out a message online to recruit a team. The ad was unusual to say the least . . .

WANTED

SCIENTISTS WITH CAVING EXPERIENCE AND EXCELLENT EXCAVATION SKILLS.
MUST BE SMALL AND NOT AFRAID OF CRAMPED SPACES.

Out of sixty applicants, six young female scientists were chosen. They came from all around the world and arrived at the Rising Star cave excited and ready for an adventure.

Marina, Becca, and Hannah went first. Video cameras underground transmitted footage to the surface, where Matt and his family were watching with bated breath.

Superman's crawl (9 in. across): Hannah wriggles forward with one arm out in front, like Superman.

The Dragon's Back: Becca scales a series of sharp ridges, like the armored plates of a mythical monster, with dizzying drops on either side.

The Chute (with a 7-inch "pinch point"): Marina shimmies down the terrifying chute. "It was like a shark's mouth," she said later. "Sharp teeth everywhere!"

The women worked for days, carefully excavating the bones and bringing them out of the cave to be examined.

Matt was overjoyed when the announcement finally came. The skeletons in the cave belonged to another undiscovered species of human ancestor. These skeletons were a little less ape-like than Karabo and a little more like humans.

Matt's dad named the species *Homo naledi*, which means "star person," because the bones were discovered in the Rising Star cave. As for the six intrepid scientists, their amazing work and impressive bravery was celebrated and they became known as "the underground astronauts!"

Some paleontologists go their whole lives without making a major discovery. Matt Berger had now been involved in not one but two, all before he even turned sixteen!

DAISY MORRIS

SPOTS A PREHISTORIC PTEROSAUR

ISLE OF WIGHT, ENGLAND, 2008

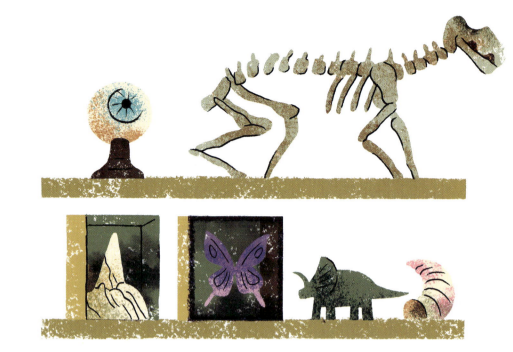

The Morris family lived on the Isle of Wight, a beautiful island known for its rugged cliffs, its pretty beaches, and, most important to Daisy Morris, its fossils!

Daisy's family loved to walk. On weekends, they would drive to the top of nearby Atherfield cliff and hike down a winding path to the beach below. More often than not, it was the youngest member of the family, Daisy, who suggested these walks. She loved any opportunity to get outside, find a fresh mudslide, and see what treasures she could add to her collection. She'd found all sorts at the beach and in the fields near her home, from amazing animal skulls and tiny bones, to ancient fossils and pretty shells. Her bedroom was starting to look like a natural history museum!

Daisy's most impressive discovery happened on a windy November morning, when she was just four and a half years old. A recent storm had caused a huge section of cliff to slide down on to the beach, and the Morris family were exploring the newly revealed layers of rock and clay. Daisy's older siblings, Lily, Poppy, and Riann, had clambered up the collapsed section of the cliff, but Daisy had chosen to search lower down, closer to the water. Her little blue bucket was already half full of natural treasures with strange and wonderful nicknames: "mermaid's purses," "devil's toenails," and "fool's gold." But something even more exciting was waiting for Daisy amongst the rocks.

"Mommy!" she shouted suddenly. "I found a bone!"

Even at the age of four, Daisy was able to recognize the honeycomb texture of fossilized bone. She wiped away some mud with her thumb, revealing a knobby shape with a circular hole in the center.

When Daisy's mom came over and looked at the fossil, she shook her head in astonishment. "It looks like a little pelvis to me," she said. "That's the bone connecting a creature's backbone to its legs. It's obviously millions of years old and I've never seen anything like it. Amazing spot, Daisy!"

Daisy's mom and dad got in touch with a fossil collector who also lived on the Isle of Wight. Martin Simpson, often known as "the Fossil Man," sat on the sofa in the Morris's cottage and stared closely at Daisy's find.

"Good job, Daisy," the Fossil Man beamed. "A few hours later and this beauty would have been taken by the tide and smashed to smithereens. You did well to leave some clay on it too, which tells me its age . . . 125 million years, give or take a few!"

"Wow!' Daisy gasped. "What kind of creature was it?"

"I don't know," the Fossil Man replied. "But I know who will!"

The Fossil Man showed Daisy's bone to Professor Darren Naish, a dinosaur expert at the University of Southampton. "Pelvis and part of a spine," said the professor, his eyes shining. "I'll need to study it some more, of course, but I think it's something special!"

Daisy and her family promised not to tell anyone about the discovery until Darren and Martin had written a scientific report. This took several years, but it was definitely worth the wait . . .

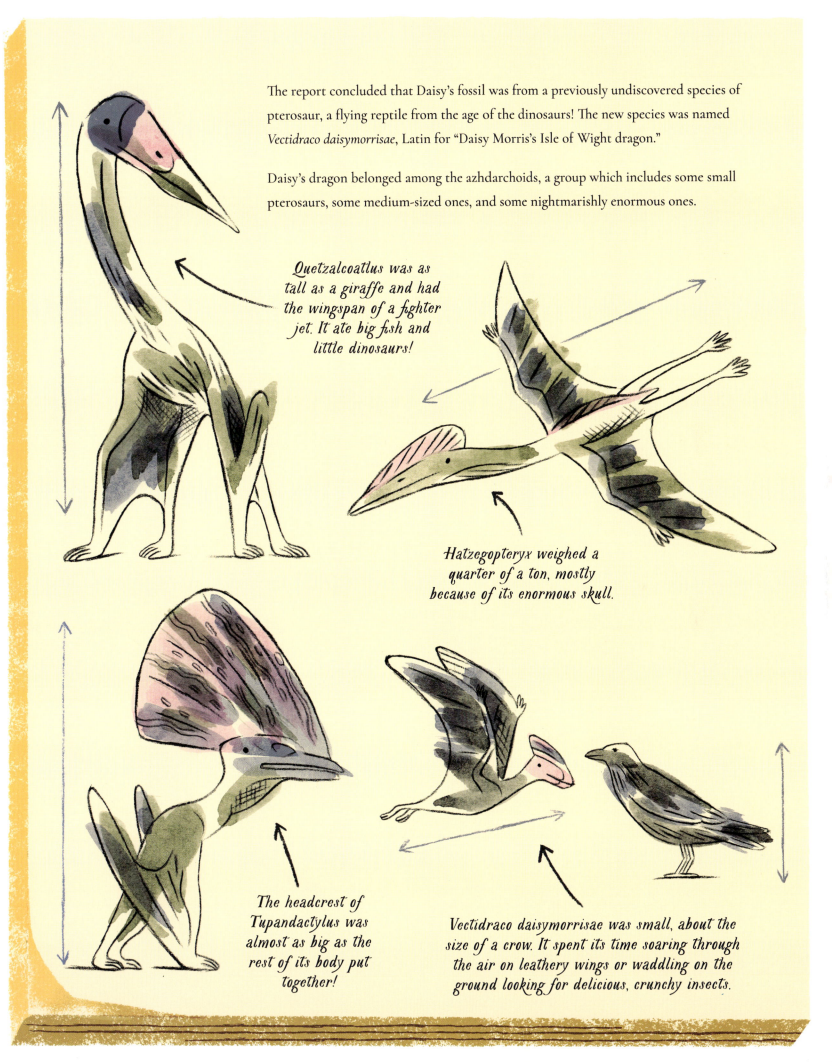

The report concluded that Daisy's fossil was from a previously undiscovered species of pterosaur, a flying reptile from the age of the dinosaurs! The new species was named *Vectidraco daisymorrisae*, Latin for "Daisy Morris's Isle of Wight dragon."

Daisy's dragon belonged among the azhdarchoids, a group which includes some small pterosaurs, some medium-sized ones, and some nightmarishly enormous ones.

Quetzalcoatlus was as tall as a giraffe and had the wingspan of a fighter jet. It ate big fish and little dinosaurs!

Hatzegopteryx weighed a quarter of a ton, mostly because of its enormous skull.

The headcrest of Tupandactylus was almost as big as the rest of its body put together!

Vectidraco daisymorrisae was small, about the size of a crow. It spent its time soaring through the air on leathery wings or waddling on the ground looking for delicious, crunchy insects.

Daisy was eight years old when her discovery finally hit the headlines. That day, the phone did not stop ringing, with reporters from all over the world asking for interviews with Daisy. It wasn't easy for a young, quiet girl to be the center of so much attention, but Daisy handled it well and shared the news of her incredible discovery on television shows like *Newsround*, *Blue Peter*, and *The One Show*.

As for the fossil, Daisy decided it belonged in a museum. She and her family were invited to the Natural History Museum in London. There, they met Dr. Lorna Steel, who looked after the pterosaur collection.

Dr. Steel took Daisy's family to a special store room and showed them the cabinet which would be Vectidraco's new home.

Daisy could hardly believe her eyes when she saw the label on the drawer right next to hers. Mary Anning, fossil hunter extraordinaire, adored the natural world just like Daisy, and was never happier than when she was scouring landslides for ancient treasures.

PV R 1034: Pterosaur bones, discovered in Lyme Regis by Miss Mary Anning.

Daisy continues to be fascinated by nature, and she still loves to go fossil hunting with her family on the weekends. She is living proof that you are never too young to make a life-changing discovery!

KATHRYN GRAY

SPIES A SUPERNOVA

———

BIRDTON, CANADA, 2011

It was the middle of a school break and ten-year-old Kathryn Aurora Gray was on a mission. She was searching the skies for something special. Not a planet, or a moon, or a boring asteroid. And not a star—or at least not your average, twinkle-twinkle kind of star that you can see any old time. No, Kathryn was searching for a supernova.

Kathryn had first learned about supernovas from her dad, who was an astronomer. He had told her that in 1054, almost a thousand years ago, Chinese stargazers noticed a new star in the night sky, much brighter than any other. But to their amazement, the star only stayed for eighteen months before disappearing completely. These astronomers didn't understand how a star could come from nowhere, stay a while, and then vanish again. It was like a kind of magic. They called it a "guest star"—here today and gone tomorrow.

Nowadays, we use the word "supernova" instead of "guest star." A supernova starts off as a star that exists far, far away from us, so far that we can't see its light. But when that star dies, the explosion is so dramatic and powerful that it becomes visible here on Earth for a while, before fading away again.

Astronomy fans hunt for undiscovered supernovas by choosing a small section of deep space and comparing two photographs of it on a computer: a new image taken recently and an old image taken a few years ago.

If they notice a bright spot in the recent photo that isn't visible in the old one, they might have found a supernova!

Kathryn was determined to find her very own supernova. She was all set up on the family computer, ready to start her hunt in Camelopardalis, a constellation shaped like a giraffe.

Five minutes passed . . . then ten . . . and then fifteen . . .

Kathryn narrowed her eyes as she flicked back and forth between new and old photos, utterly engrossed.

"Dad," she said suddenly. "Is this one?"

Kathryn's dad looked where she was pointing. A pinprick of light was blinking at him, and he blinked back at it, amazed. Astronomers spend years hunting for supernovas. Surely Kathryn could not have spotted one in fifteen minutes!

"Yup," he said cautiously. "That looks good."

"Woohoo!" Kathryn cheered, thrusting both fists into the air.

The very next day, the Royal Astronomical Society of Canada confirmed that Kathryn's discovery was indeed a supernova, 240 million light years from Earth.

Kathryn became famous overnight as the youngest person ever to discover a supernova. The whole world wanted to hear about her unusual hobby and the weeks that followed were a blur of excitement. Kathryn's proudest moment was giving a speech at an astronomy event. She walked onstage and talked about her passion for space. The audience was full of famous people, including the one and only Neil Armstrong, the first man ever to walk on the Moon. Kathryn even got a selfie with him!

Inspired by her discovery, Kathryn went on to study astrophysics in college, learning more about stars, supernovas, and our place in the cosmos. In a universe so breathtakingly vast, just think of all the beauty and wonder that remains to be found!

ZHENYA SALINDER

SNIFFS OUT A WOOLLY MAMMOTH

———

SIBERIA, RUSSIA, 2012

Way up north in the Arctic Circle, the River Yenisei flowed out into the icy Kara Sea. Three brothers and two sisters huddled together on the shore, while their dogs nosed about in a pile of driftwood. The children's parents had gone in search of food and would be back tomorrow.

"The cranes are flying south," said the eldest, Zhenya, glancing up at the sky. "Winter is coming." He was only eleven but he had the wise, serious face of a much older boy.

It was August and the banks of the river were covered in moss and fluffy cotton grass. But in a few weeks, the water would freeze over and the land would once again be blanketed in white.

"What's that stench?" said Zhenya suddenly.

"It's you!" giggled his little sister Neko.

"No, it's not!" Zhenya wrinkled his nose and stood up. "It smells like rotting reindeer meat, only different."

Zhenya set off along the sandy shore. His younger siblings trudged after him and the dogs ran ahead, their nostrils twitching.

"Look!" said Neko. "The dogs can smell it too!"

The children passed an abandoned army base teetering on the cliff edge. Zhenya could remember when those huts stood proudly on solid ground, but the Arctic tides were higher and warmer every year, eating away at the frosty shoreline.

The smell was getting stronger with each step they took. Zhenya looked at the frozen sandbank to his left and noticed two huge gray shapes poking out of the frost.

The dogs bounded up the slope and began digging with their front paws.

"They've found something!" cried Neko. "Looks like the heels of a sled!"

Zhenya scrambled up after the dogs, covering his nose to block the stench.

"You're right about heels!" he shouted down. "But it's definitely not a sled!"

At the Sopkarga weather station in the far north of Siberia, two polar explorers named Alexei and Sergey were engrossed in a late-night game of backgammon when a loud knock at the door broke their concentration.

The two men looked at each other, puzzled. They never had visitors up here, hundreds of miles from anywhere. Even their food delivery only came once a year, and that wasn't due for another nine months.

"Expecting someone?" Sergey asked with a smirk.

Alexei went and opened the door. He saw the glorious Northern Lights shimmering across the sky—and five children shivering on the doorstep!

The explorer ushered the siblings inside and gave them mugs of hot black tea to warm them up. "These are the children of my friend, Vadim," Alexei told Sergei. "Zhenya here is a real trooper. I once saw him pilot a heavy boat all alone on a stormy sea, hauling in his fishing nets."

"My parents were off hunting," Zhenya said with a shrug. "Someone had to feed the little ones."

"Strong as an musk ox, and modest too." Alexei grinned. "Anyway, Zhenya, what brings you here on this cold night?"

The boy put down his mug and looked the explorer in the eye. "We've found a woolly mammoth in the melting ice," he said. "We need to use your radio transmitter."

That radio message changed everything. A team of scientists traveled 3,000 miles across Russia to smoke the mammoth out of the ice, then flew it by helicopter back to their laboratory. They nicknamed the mammoth Zhenya, in honor of its discoverer.

Mammoth tusks had been found before in the Arctic, but Zhenya the mammoth was more than just a tusk. The whole gigantic skeleton was there, as well as skin, fat, meat, one ear, and one eye. It was one of the best-preserved mammoths ever discovered, providing scientists with all sorts of information about the long-extinct creature. They found out, for example, that the mammoth lived 48,000 years ago and that the hump on his back was made of fat, just like a camel's.

Zhenya the mammoth was eventually brought back to the Arctic and placed in a museum, where visitors can still see him today. As for Zhenya the boy, he was declared a hero. The local governor presented him with a certificate of honor and a cell phone as a reward.

Although Zhenya enjoyed his moment of fame—and his new phone—there was also a less positive side to his incredible discovery. With every mammoth that emerges from the permafrost, we're reminded that the ice of the Arctic is melting. This causes sea levels to rise around the world, which in turn leads to flooding and hurricanes. Zhenya's amazing find should inspire us and the adults in charge to do everything we can to fight climate change and keep our planet healthy, even if it means we'd find fewer woolly mammoths.

SAGA VANECEK

PULLS A SWORD FROM A LAKE

———

LAKE VIDÖSTERN, SWEDEN, 2018

On a scorching summer day in the south of Sweden, an eight-year-old girl named Saga was standing knee-deep in a lake, holding a smooth, flat pebble. She was on vacation with her family and was loving every minute.

Curling her index finger around the pebble's oval edge, Saga drew back her arm, then whipped it forward, hard and low.

Blip! Blip! Blip! Bloop!

The stone skipped lightly across the glittering surface of the lake, then vanished, leaving only ripples. Three bounces, Saga thought. Not bad.

"Saga!" Her Dad was beginning to get impatient. "Time to come out, the match is starting soon!"

It was the day of the World Cup final between France and Croatia. Soccer fans from every country were waiting eagerly to see which of the two superstar teams would lift the trophy.

Saga did not share her father's love of soccer. She crouched down in the lake, relishing the feel of the cool water lapping around her shoulders. Then she began to crawl forward on her hands and knees, searching for her next stone—a smooth one, flat enough for four or maybe even five skips.

"Saga, please! It's the World Cup final, it only happens once every four years!"

The little girl stopped crawling and furrowed her brow. She could feel something strange underneath her right hand and knee, something much longer and rougher than a pebble. What could it be? A broken tree branch, perhaps?

Saga pried the mysterious object out of the silt and lifted it up through the water. There was some sort of handle on one end, so she gripped it firmly and thrust it high into the air above her head.

A high-pitched voice rang out over the waters of the lake. "Daddy! I found a sword!"

It was dirty and covered in brown rust, but Saga didn't mind. Brandishing her sword that summer afternoon, she felt strangely powerful, like a warrior.

In the World Cup final, France beat Croatia by two goals to one, but Saga's dad didn't watch a single kick. He was too excited about his daughter's discovery.

Other people were excited too. "I've got goosebumps," exclaimed an archaeologist when she examined the sword the following day. "It's definitely more than 1,000 years old. I've never seen anything like it!"

Experts think that Saga's sword was thrown into the lake sometime in the Iron Age, as an offering to the Norse gods. We can only imagine who its owner might have been, and the fierce battles he or she might have fought with it.

Today the sword is in a museum in Sweden, alongside a specially made Lego figure of Saga herself. The Lego figure is holding up a tiny replica of the ancient weapon and smiling from ear to ear. What a wonderful tribute to a truly incredible discovery!

FORGOTTEN DISCOVERERS

Just like some of the children in this book, many young discoverers are met with worldwide recognition when their stories become public. Sadly, there are others who receive no credit for their finds, let alone any reward. They are forgotten or ignored, often because of their young age or even the color of their skin. Here are two examples of amazing discoveries made by children whose full names have been lost to time.

In 1952, a Scottish schoolboy was given an unusual punishment for bad behavior—an afternoon with the school gardener, digging up potatoes. The boy unearthed what he thought was just another potato, but to his surprise it was actually the head of an ancient Egyptian statue. The statue had been buried during Victorian times, possibly due to fears of an ancient curse bringing misfortune.

The boy wiped the artifact clean and took it to his locker, but a teacher heard about his find and confiscated it. The teacher donated the artifact to a museum in Edinburgh, without even telling the boy what he had done. As for the boy, he was never celebrated for his impressive discovery.

In the early 1980s, in a central African country called Zaire (now the Democratic Republic of Congo), an eight-year-old girl was playing in a pile of rubble outside her uncle's house when she found a brownish-yellow rock. Her uncle sold it to a gem dealer, who identified it as an enormous diamond.

Once cut, the diamond became known as the "Incomparable Diamond" and later as the "Golden Canary" because of its incredible size and color. It went on a glamorous world tour to Dubai, Taipei, Geneva, Hong Kong, and finally New York, where it sold at auction for a whopping $12.4 million.

The girl herself received none of the fame or fortune that should have been hers.

There are likely many more young discoverers out there, whose achievements have never been recognized. So, if you discover something wonderful, be sure to share your story far and wide!

TOMORROW'S TREASURE

All over the world, there are discoveries waiting to happen. Who knows what wondrous finds will hit the headlines in the years to come and who will be the lucky discoverers. Here are three examples of treasure that we know is out there, itching to be found . . .

KING JOHN'S LOST TREASURE

On October 12, 1216, King John of England was riding across a sandy bay when the tide rushed in, turning the ground to deadly quicksand. The king escaped but his oxcarts were sucked under, along with his crown, his jewels, a casket of gold coins, and a priceless sword. The treasure has never been recovered.

DINOSAUR BONES

Paleontology in the twenty-first century is a thrilling, fast-moving roller coaster ride. On average, a new species of dinosaur is named every two weeks, and scientists believe there are thousands and maybe millions more species yet to be found.

FABERGÉ EGGS

Over a hundred years ago, a jeweler named Peter Fabergé made fifty-two extraordinary Easter eggs for the empresses of Russia. Each creation was crafted not from chocolate but from gold, rubies, and diamonds. Forty-five of these beauties are in museums and millionaires' mansions. Another recently turned up in a rummage sale. The other six are missing . . . at least for now.

WHAT IF I'M THE NEXT YOUNG DISCOVERER?

You know the old saying "finders keepers?" It's not always true. If you unearth something special, there are a few rules to keep in mind.

Any discovery of real historical importance belongs in a museum, where it can be studied by scientists and enjoyed by visitors. If a museum wants to put your find in their collection, they should pay you a fair price for it.

Never take an artifact out of its country of origin. This is a form of stealing, even if it ends up in a museum.

If you find a stash of old coins, or anything containing gold or silver, this classes as "treasure." Different countries have different laws about whether treasure belongs to the finder, the government, or the person who owns the land it was found on. Even if you don't get to keep your treasure, you will almost certainly receive a reward for finding it!

If you find a new species of animal—alive, extinct, or prehistoric—don't forget to report it. It could end up being named after you!

What are you waiting for? Get out there and get discovering!

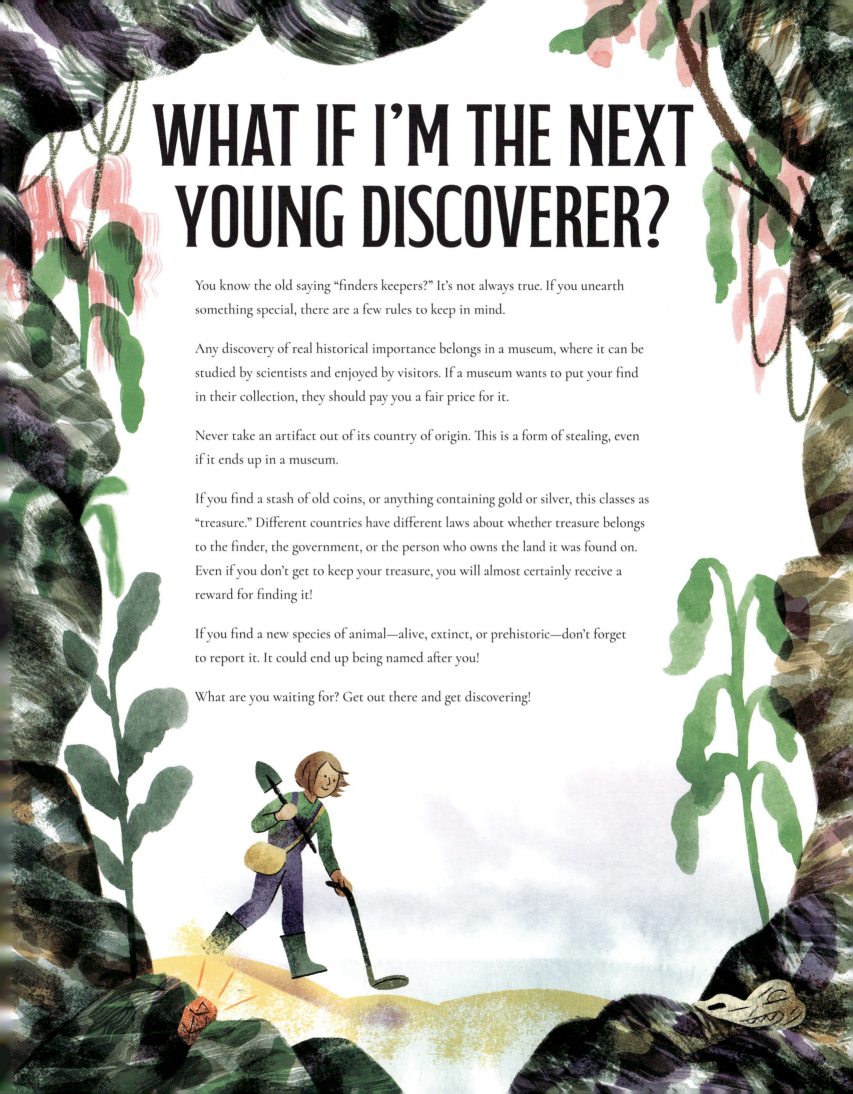

GLOSSARY

Archaeology: The study of ancient objects like tools, pottery, and buildings. Archaeologists dig in the ground to find these things and learn about how people used to live.

Assyria: An ancient kingdom in what is now Northern Iraq, known for its amazing buildings and its powerful army.

Carat: The measure of a gemstone's weight. The more carats a gem weighs, the more valuable it is. (Not to be confused with "carrot.")

Fossil: The hard remains of a plant or animal that lived long ago, often found in rock.

Geology: The study of rocks, sand, and soil.

Paleontology: The study of animals and plants that lived millions of years ago.

Prehistory: The time before people wrote things down. We learn about prehistory by studying objects, fossils, and other clues.

Profit: The extra money you make after selling something for more than it cost you.

Shale: Soft, crumbly rock made from mud or clay. Sometimes contains fossils!

Treasure: In everyday speech, treasure could be any exciting find. But in archaeology, treasure refers to objects made of gold or silver.